contents

NZ, Canada, US and UK readers
Please note: Australian cup and spoon measurements are metric. A conversion chart appears on page 62.

perfect cocktails – tips & tricks

*Whether you're throwing a drinks party or merely mixing a quiet tipple,
the following tips will ensure that you're equipped and informed –
and the perfect cocktail can be yours.*

equipment

Behind every good host stands a great blender. You'll need one that is powerful
enough to crush ice. You'll also need a cocktail shaker, a strainer, cocktail measuring
equipment, a mortar and pestle, swizzle sticks, straws and an assortment of glasses.

general tips

- Since ice is a primary ingredient in many cocktails, it should be handled accordingly. Take it out of the freezer just before using to ensure it is dry. To crush ice, start the blender on low until the ice begins to crush, then switch to high speed. Alternatively, place ice in a clean tea towel or plastic bag and crush with a meat mallet, rolling pin or hammer. If possible, try to use ice that has been freshly made – ice that remains in the freezer, uncovered, can absorb the smells and flavours of other food stored in the freezer.

- The quality of the liquor makes a world of difference. Nothing will mask second-rate alcohol.
- We have specified if fresh juice is required; otherwise, use bottled juice from the supermarket. If a recipe calls for concentrated juice, do not substitute fresh juice, as it is too watery.
- Freeze fresh fruit to make a smoother, less watery drink. For best results, prepare fruit the same day by cutting into chunks, then laying chunks flat in the freezer in a plastic bag. Depending on the variety of fruit, the pieces will be ready in 30 minutes to 1 hour.

techniques

salting or sugaring glass rims

Rub the flesh of a lime or lemon around the
rim of your chosen glass until the whole rim
has been evenly moistened with juice. Turn
the glass upside down and dip the rim into
a saucer filled with salt or caster sugar.
Shake away any excess seasoning.

basic recipes

sugar syrup

Sugar syrup, often called gomme syrup, is used for sweetening drinks.

Combine 1 cup (220g) sugar and 1 cup (250ml) water in a small saucepan; stir over low heat until sugar dissolves. Bring to a boil, then reduce heat and simmer, uncovered, without stirring, 5 minutes; remove from heat, cool. Store in an airtight container in the refrigerator for up to 2 months.
makes about 350ml

sour mix

Sour mix is also known as sweet and sour mix or bar mix.

Combine 1 quantity (350ml) sugar syrup (see recipe above), 120ml lemon or lime juice and 1 egg white (this is optional, but will make the drinks slightly foamy). Store in an airtight container in the refrigerator for up to 3 days.
makes about 470ml

hot and sour mix

Combine 120ml sour mix (see previous recipe) with 4 halved fresh red thai chillies (seeds included). Stir and refrigerate for up to 3 days. Strain before using.
makes about 120ml

mint syrup

Fill a large bowl with ice and water. Bring a small saucepan of water to a boil. Plunge 2 cups firmly packed fresh mint leaves into boiling water for about 3 seconds. Remove with a slotted spoon, then immediately transfer to iced water until cold; drain. Combine 180ml sugar syrup (see earlier recipe) and mint in a blender jug; blend until pureed, stand syrup for 10 minutes. Push syrup through a fine sieve, pressing down firmly to extract as much liquid from mint as possible, discard mint pulp. Store in an airtight container for up to 1 week in the refrigerator.
makes about 180ml

muddling fruit for "stick" drinks

A muddler is a thick wooden "stick". In this book, we used a mortar and pestle instead; if you own a muddler, though, use it rather than a pestle. To muddle fruit, eg, lime wedges, place lime in tumbler or cocktail shaker then, using muddler, press heavily on lime with a mashing motion. Use crush of fruit and juice, unstrained, in the cocktail.

simple & elegant cocktail food

When you're concentrating on making sure the cocktails are just right, you don't need the extra pressure of cooking. These easy ideas for finger food will come to your rescue – be sure to serve them bite-sized.

Wrap prosciutto around grissini (bread sticks) and serve with green olive tapenade.

Diagonally halve store-bought fresh Vietnamese spring rolls and serve with separate dipping bowls of hoisin sauce, sweet chilli sauce, and fish sauce laced with fine slices of chilli.

- Serve store-bought sushi with dipping bowls of tamari and wasabi paste.

- Top toasted rounds of French bread with rare roast beef, horseradish cream and baby rocket leaves.

- Heat frozen potato wedges until crisp and hot; serve with bowls of sweet chilli sauce, and sour cream and chives.

- Top thin slices of pumpernickel with smoked salmon, dill sprigs and a quick squeeze of lemon juice.

- Toss cashews and peanuts in a mix of butter, dried chilli flakes, sea salt, ground cumin and ground coriander, then roast in the oven until golden.

Serve elegant fingers of crustless sandwiches; try finely sliced cucumber, mayonnaise and dill as a filling, or a combination of shredded chicken, toasted flaked almonds, celery and mayonnaise.

After the party, serve small cups of strong black coffee accompanied by halved fresh figs that have been drizzled with top-quality honey.

- Serve slices of Turkish bread with store-bought dips (choose between hummus, baba ghanoush, tzatziki, taramasalata, etc).

- Toss green and black olives with a mix of chopped fresh herbs (basil, oregano, thyme and rosemary) and serve in bowls.

- Lay out a platter containing the best of the season's produce: include luscious stone fruit, berries and thin slices of melon in the warmer months; in the cooler months try blood oranges, fresh dates, dried muscatel grapes, paper-thin slices of pear and apple, brie and wafer biscuits.

fresca

Prediction: the next wave of the ever-growing cocktail craze will include this drink.

1 medium grapefruit,
   cut into 8 wedges
1 tablespoon palm sugar
   or brown sugar
1 cup ice cubes
45ml vodka
10ml sugar syrup
   (see page 3)
120ml lemonade

Using a mortar and pestle (or muddler), crush the grapefruit and sugar together.
Place ice in glass; add grapefruit mixture and remaining ingredients, stir.
glass 300ml highball
garnish a straw

cosmopolitan

10ml citron vodka
20ml vodka
30ml Cointreau
60ml cranberry juice
10ml fresh lime juice
1 cup ice cubes

Combine ingredients
in a cocktail shaker.
Shake vigorously then
strain into chilled glass.
glass 150ml cocktail
garnish twist of lime rind

salty dog

1 cup ice cubes
45ml vodka
120ml fresh
    grapefruit juice

Place ice in salt-rimmed
(see page 2) glass;
add vodka then juice.
glass 300ml highball
garnish grapefruit rind knot

cajun bloody mary

The classic morning-after eye-opener. To make chilli-infused vodka, combine 250ml vodka and 4 fresh red thai chillies in a glass jar, cover; stand for about 5 days or until the vodka is infused with chilli heat. Discard chillies before using.

1 cup ice cubes
30ml chilli-infused vodka
10ml fresh lemon juice
dash worcestershire sauce
dash Tabasco sauce
pinch celery salt
pinch cracked
    black pepper
120ml tomato juice

Combine ice, vodka, lemon juice and sauces in glass rimmed (see page 2) with celery salt and pepper; add tomato juice, stir.

glass 300ml highball
garnish lemon wedge and two straws

9

caipiroska

This contemporary take on the traditional Brazilian caipirinha is a concoction of vodka, fresh limes, sugar and ice. In bars, it is often prepared using a wooden tool called a muddler (see page 3), but you can make it at home using a mortar and pestle.

1 lime, cut into 8 wedges
1 tablespoon palm sugar
   or brown sugar
60ml vodka
10ml sugar syrup
   (see page 3)
½ cup ice cubes
½ cup crushed ice

Using a mortar and pestle (or muddler), crush 6 lime wedges with the sugar. **Combine** lime mixture in a cocktail shaker with vodka, sugar syrup and ice cubes. Shake vigorously then pour into glass with crushed ice; do not strain.
glass 180ml old-fashioned
garnish remaining lime wedges and two straws

watermelon caipiroska

1 lime, cut into 8 wedges
1 teaspoon sugar
10ml sugar syrup
(see page 3)
4 x 5cm pieces
watermelon
45ml vodka
15ml watermelon liqueur
½ cup ice cubes
½ cup crushed ice

Using a mortar and pestle (or muddler), crush 6 lime wedges with sugar, sugar syrup and watermelon.
Combine watermelon mixture in a cocktail shaker with vodka, watermelon liqueur and ice cubes. Shake vigorously then pour into glass with crushed ice; do not strain.
glass 180ml old-fashioned
garnish remaining lime wedges, a swizzle stick and a straw

11

lemon friatto

30ml citron vodka
30ml limoncello
1 teaspoon finely grated
     orange rind
1 cup ice cubes
3 medium scoops
     lemon sorbet

Combine vodka,
limoncello, rind and ice
cubes in a cocktail
shaker; shake vigorously.
Place sorbet in chilled
glass; pour limoncello
mixture over the sorbet.
glass 150ml cocktail
garnish thin strips of
lemon rind and a straw

atlantic passion

We used canned passionfruit in syrup, available from supermarkets. To make fresh strawberry juice, blend or process 250g fresh strawberries, then push through a fine sieve. We rimmed the cocktail glass with pink sugar; simply add a drop of red food colouring to sugar and mix well.

30ml vodka
60ml fresh
   strawberry puree
15ml passionfruit in syrup
10ml sugar syrup
   (see page 3)
1 cup ice cubes

Combine ingredients in a cocktail shaker. Shake vigorously then strain into chilled sugar-rimmed (see page 2) glass.
glass 150ml cocktail
garnish twist of orange rind

sea breeze

In this recipe, you can substitute fresh grapefruit juice for the ruby red grapefruit juice if the ruby red variety is not available.

120ml cranberry juice
30ml ruby red
   grapefruit juice
45ml vodka
1 cup ice cubes

Combine ingredients in glass, stir well.
glass 300ml highball
garnish two straws

redskin

To make vanilla-infused vodka, combine 250ml vodka and 2 split vanilla beans in a glass jar, cover; stand for about 5 days or until the vodka is infused with vanilla flavour. Discard vanilla beans before using the vodka. Guava juice is available from most supermarkets and delicatessens.

45ml vanilla-infused vodka
30ml strawberry liqueur
120ml bottled guava juice
6 fresh strawberries
1 cup ice cubes

Combine ingredients in jug of a blender; blend on high speed until smooth, pour into glass.
glass 300ml highball
garnish twist of red-apple skin and a straw

black russian

Tia Maria or dark crème de cacao can be substituted for Kahlua.

½ cup ice cubes
30ml vodka
30ml Kahlua
120ml cola, optional

Place ice in glass; pour vodka then Kahlua over ice. Top with cola, if desired.

glass 180ml old-fashioned
garnish a straw

white russian

½ cup ice cubes
30ml vodka
30ml Kahlua
30ml fresh cream

Place ice in glass;
pour vodka then
Kahlua over ice.
Gently pour cream into
glass over the back of
a tablespoon so cream
floats. Do not stir.

glass 180ml old-fashioned
garnish a straw

long island iced tea

1 cup ice cubes
30ml vodka
30ml tequila
30ml Bacardi
30ml gin
15ml Cointreau
15ml fresh lemon juice
15ml sugar syrup
    (see page 3)
30ml cola

Place ice in glass; add
vodka, tequila, Bacardi,
gin and Cointreau, one
after the other.
Add juice and syrup,
top with cola; stir.

glass 300ml highball
garnish twist of lemon rind,
mint leaves, swizzle stick
and a straw

flirtini

6 fresh raspberries
1 cup ice cubes
30ml vodka
15ml Cointreau
15ml cranberry juice
15ml fresh lime juice
15ml bottled
    pineapple juice
60ml brut champagne

Crush raspberries in base of chilled glass; top with half of the ice.
Combine remaining ice, vodka, Cointreau and juices in a cocktail shaker. Shake vigorously then strain into glass; top with champagne.

glass 300ml highball
garnish extra fresh raspberries threaded onto a toothpick and balanced across rim of glass

vanilla martini

To make vanilla-infused vodka, combine 250ml vodka and 2 split vanilla beans in a glass jar, cover; stand for about 5 days or until the vodka is infused with vanilla flavour. Discard vanilla beans before using vodka.

45ml vanilla-infused vodka
10ml sugar syrup
(see page 3)
15ml Frangelico
1 cup ice cubes

Combine ingredients in a cocktail shaker. Shake vigorously then strain into chilled glass.
glass 90ml martini

chocolate martini

10ml chocolate Ice Magic
1 cup ice cubes
45ml vodka
20ml white crème
  de cacao
45ml chocolate liqueur
10ml raspberry liqueur
20ml Baileys

Using Ice Magic, trace outline of a 9cm-circle (or the diameter of the glass rim) on a flat plate; working quickly, twist the rim of glass in Ice Magic before it sets. Briefly place glass upright in freezer to set chocolate.

Combine half of the ice, vodka and crème de cacao in a cocktail shaker. Shake vigorously then strain into glass.

Combine remaining ice, liqueurs and Baileys in cocktail shaker. Shake vigorously then pour gently into glass over the back of a tablespoon so mixture floats. Do not stir.

glass 150ml cocktail
garnish grated chocolate and a raspberry

21

apple martini

45ml vodka
30ml apple schnapps
5ml sugar syrup
   (see page 3)
1 cup ice cubes

Combine ingredients in
a cocktail shaker. Shake
vigorously then strain
into chilled glass.
glass 90ml martini
garnish sliver of green apple

dry martini

The best-known of the classic cocktails, the Martini seems simple in its composition yet there are endless subtle variations. The critical factor in a Martini is its dryness, so the amount of vermouth added is very important.

45ml gin
15ml dry vermouth
1 cup ice cubes

Combine ingredients in a cocktail shaker. Shake vigorously then strain into chilled glass.

glass 90ml martini
garnish a caperberry

sweet martini

45ml gin
15ml vermouth rosso
1 cup ice cubes

Combine ingredients in
a cocktail shaker. Shake
vigorously then strain
into a chilled glass.
glass 90ml martini
garnish a maraschino cherry

negroni

For a longer, sweeter drink, omit the lemon rind from this recipe and top the drink up with 30ml soda water.

1 cup ice cubes
5cm piece lemon rind
45ml gin
30ml vermouth rosso
45ml Campari

Place ice and rind in glass; pour gin, vermouth and Campari over ice, one after the other.

glass 180ml old-fashioned
garnish a straw

campari lady

For a sweeter drink, use bottled ruby red grapefruit juice instead of fresh grapefruit juice.

30ml gin
45ml Campari
120ml fresh grapefruit juice
30ml tonic water
1 cup ice cubes

Combine ingredients in a cocktail shaker. Shake vigorously then strain into glass with some of the ice.
glass 300ml highball
garnish two straws

fallen angel

One version of the Fallen Angel cocktail is made with crème de menthe, but this version, using blue curaçao, is more popular with us.

75ml gin
40ml blue curaçao
25ml fresh lemon juice
dash Angostura bitters
1 cup ice cubes
100ml lemonade

Combine gin, blue curaçao, juice and bitters in glass; add ice, top with lemonade.

glass 350ml piña colada
garnish a straw and a swizzle stick

fruit collins

While the Tom Collins is the classic, don't let that put you off the other delicious, thirst-quenching variations. For this recipe, you will need to blend about a 10cm-chunk of watermelon then pour it through a sieve to catch the seeds.

1 cup ice cubes
45ml ruby red
   grapefruit juice
45ml fresh
   watermelon juice
30ml fresh lime juice
10ml sugar syrup
   (see page 3)
60ml gin
60ml soda water

Place ice in glass; add juices and syrup, one at a time, then gin. Stir, top with soda water; stir again.
glass 300ml highball (pictured in background)
garnish thin slice of lime and two straws

mudslide shake

20ml chocolate Ice Magic
1 cup crushed ice
30ml vodka
30ml Baileys
30ml Kahlua
30ml thickened cream
2 medium scoops
   vanilla ice-cream
1 medium scoop
   chocolate ice-cream

Drizzle Ice Magic around inside of glass; place glass upright in freezer for 5 minutes to set.
Meanwhile, combine ice, vodka, Baileys, Kahlua and cream in jug of a blender; blend on high speed briefly.
Add ice cream; blend on low speed until just combined, pour into glass.

glass 400ml fountain
garnish a straw

cherish

8 fresh or canned cherries,
   seeded and halved
15ml cherry brandy
15ml Malibu
15ml Frangelico
15ml raspberry liqueur
30ml fresh cream
½ cup ice cubes

Place cherries in jug of
a blender; blend on low
speed until crushed.
Combine cherries with
remaining ingredients in
a cocktail shaker. Shake
vigorously then strain
into chilled glass.
glass 150ml cocktail
garnish dark chocolate
curls and a straw

red corvette

We rimmed the cocktail glass with pink sugar; simply add a drop of red food colouring to sugar and mix well.

45ml Frangelico
30ml Midori
4 fresh strawberries
1 cup ice cubes

Combine ingredients in jug of a blender; blend on high speed until well combined, pour into chilled sugar-rimmed (see page 2) glass.

glass 150ml cocktail
garnish a straw

toblerone

5ml honey
10ml chocolate Ice Magic
30ml Frangelico
30ml Kahlua
30ml Baileys
15ml dark crème de cacao
60ml fresh cream
1 cup ice cubes

Drizzle honey and
Ice Magic around inside
of chilled glass; place
glass upright in freezer
for 5 minutes to set.
Combine remaining
ingredients in jug of
a blender; blend until
well combined, pour
into glass.
glass 150ml cocktail
garnish crushed Flake
chocolate bar and a straw

baileys crunch

2 Oreo biscuits
60ml Baileys
30ml dark crème de cacao
30ml chocolate liqueur
1 cup crushed ice

Pull biscuits apart, remove white filling; crush biscuits with rolling pin or meat mallet.

Combine remaining ingredients in a cocktail shaker. Shake vigorously then pour into chilled glass; sprinkle with crushed biscuits.

glass 150ml cocktail
garnish a straw

bounty

We used Monin coconut syrup for this cocktail, available from delicatessens and liquor shops.

30ml Baileys
15ml Kahlua
15ml coconut syrup
60ml fresh cream
1 cup ice cubes

Combine ingredients in jug of a blender; blend on high speed until well combined, pour into glass.
glass 180ml brandy balloon
garnish pineapple leaf and a straw

mai tai

1 cup ice cubes
30ml Bacardi
30ml dark rum
15ml orange curaçao
15ml Amaretto
15ml fresh lemon juice
15ml sugar syrup
   (see page 3)
15ml fresh orange juice
15ml bottled
   pineapple juice
10ml grenadine

Place ice in glass; pour remaining ingredients, except grenadine, one at a time over ice, stir gently. Carefully add grenadine.

glass 300ml pilsener
garnish a pineapple slice, a maraschino cherry and a straw

piña colada

45ml Bacardi
120ml bottled
   pineapple juice
30ml coconut cream
15ml Malibu
15ml sugar syrup
   (see page 3)
1 cup ice cubes

Combine ingredients in
jug of a blender; blend
on high speed until
smooth. Pour into glass.
glass 400ml tulip-shaped
garnish two pineapple
leaves and two straws

planter's punch

Bacardi or dark rum can be used, though the slightly darker rum has a stronger flavour.

1 cup ice cubes
50ml Bacardi
25ml fresh lime juice
20ml lime juice cordial
dash Angostura bitters
30ml soda water

Combine ice, Bacardi, juice, cordial and bitters in a cocktail shaker. Shake vigorously, then pour mixture into a glass; top with chilled soda water, stir.
glass 300ml highball
garnish a straw

scorpion

45ml dark rum
30ml Bacardi
30ml brandy
15ml Cointreau
90ml fresh orange juice
1 cup ice cubes
15ml fresh lime juice

Combine rum, Bacardi, brandy, Cointreau, orange juice and half of the ice in a cocktail shaker. Shake vigorously then pour into a glass; add remaining ice and lime juice, stir.
glass 300ml highball
garnish a straw

traditional daiquiri

The Daiquiri was created in a small Cuban town of the same name by an American engineer, who combined the local spirit (rum) with native limes to make the ultimate pick-me-up after a hot day in the iron mines.

45ml Bacardi
30ml fresh lime juice
15ml sugar syrup
   (see page 3)
1 cup ice cubes

Combine ingredients in a cocktail shaker. Shake vigorously then strain into a glass.
glass 150ml cocktail

39

frozen mango daiquiri

To make this granita-like concoction, we recommend blending the ice with the mango for about 20 seconds, alternating between low and high speed, before adding the other ingredients. Don't make this drink too far in advance because it can become watery.

60ml Bacardi
60ml mango liqueur
30ml fresh lime juice
1 medium ripe
   mango, peeled,
   chopped coarsely
1 cup ice cubes

Combine ingredients in jug of a blender; blend until just combined, pour into glass.
glass 300ml highball

passionfruit and pineapple daiquiri

*We used canned
passionfruit in syrup
for this cocktail,
which is available
from supermarkets.*

45ml Bacardi
30ml passionfruit in syrup
30ml bottled
     pineapple juice
15ml Cointreau
15ml fresh lime juice
1 cup ice cubes

Combine ingredients in
a cocktail shaker. Shake
vigorously then strain into
a chilled glass.
glass 150ml cocktail
garnish a pineapple spear

sade lemonade

1 cup ice cubes
30ml scotch whisky
30ml Midori
50ml bottled apple juice
60ml ginger beer
60ml lemonade

Half-fill a glass with
ice. Pour remaining
ingredients, one after the
other, over ice; stir gently.
glass 300ml highball
garnish a slice of lemon
and a straw

manhattan

Another classic, and perhaps the best known of all the whisky cocktails. Rye and bourbon are preferred to scotch whisky in this recipe; sweet vermouth is believed to blend better with whiskies than dry.

60ml rye whisky
30ml vermouth rosso
1 cup ice cubes

Combine ingredients in a cocktail shaker. Shake vigorously then strain into a chilled glass.

glass 150ml margarita
garnish a maraschino cherry dropped in the glass

brandy alexander

45ml brandy
30ml dark crème de cacao
60ml fresh cream
1 cup ice cubes

Combine ingredients in a cocktail shaker. Shake vigorously then strain into a glass.
glass 150ml cocktail
garnish cross two straws over the rim of glass; lightly sprinkle ground nutmeg over surface of drink, remove straws carefully

illusion

45ml Midori
20ml Cointreau
20ml vodka
60ml bottled
    pineapple juice
20ml fresh lime juice
1 cup ice cubes

Combine ingredients in
a cocktail shaker. Shake
vigorously then strain
into a glass.
glass 240ml red wine
garnish thin slices of lime

mint julep

This cocktail should be made with the best bourbon you can buy.

30ml mint syrup
  (see page 3)
60ml bourbon
2 cups ice cubes

Pour 10ml of the mint syrup into a chilled glass.
Combine bourbon and ice in jug of a blender, blend until smooth.
Spoon bourbon mixture into glass; stir, drizzle with remaining mint syrup.
glass 300ml highball
garnish a straw

frozen tequila sunrise

30ml tequila
90ml orange juice
   concentrate, frozen
1¹/₂ cups ice cubes
10ml grenadine

Combine tequila,
juice and ice in jug of
a blender; blend until
smooth, pour into glass.
Carefully drizzle
grenadine, over the back
of a tablespoon, around
inside rim of glass.
glass 300ml highball
garnish a straw

margarita

You can use triple sec or white curaçao instead of Cointreau, if you prefer.

45ml tequila
30ml fresh lime juice
30ml Cointreau
1 cup ice cubes

Combine ingredients in a cocktail shaker. Shake vigorously then strain into a salt-rimmed (see page 2) glass.
glass 150ml margarita
garnish a slice of lemon

frozen strawberry margarita

30ml tequila
15ml Cointreau
15ml strawberry liqueur
30ml fresh lime juice
4 frozen strawberries
1 cup ice cubes

Combine ingredients
in jug of a blender;
blend until smooth. Pour
mixture into salt-rimmed
(see page 2) glass.
glass 150ml margarita
garnish a strawberry wedge

imperial margarita

45ml tequila
30ml orange curaçao
30ml Cointreau
15ml fresh lime juice
1 cup ice cubes

Combine ingredients in
a cocktail shaker. Shake
vigorously then strain
into a salt-rimmed
(see page 2) glass.
glass 150ml margarita

chilli margarita

For a frozen chilli margarita, blend ingredients together in jug of a blender then pour into a cocktail glass.

20ml tequila
10ml Cointreau
45ml hot and sour mix
    (see page 3)
dash Tabasco sauce
1 cup ice cubes

Combine ingredients in a cocktail shaker. Shake vigorously then strain into a glass.

glass 150ml margarita
garnish A slice of lime and a curled fresh red chilli

pineapple and mint margarita

30ml tequila
15ml Cointreau
30ml fresh lime juice
30ml bottled
    pineapple juice
4 fresh mint leaves
1 cup ice cubes

Combine ingredients in
jug of a blender; blend
on high speed until well
combined. Pour mixture
into a salt-rimmed
(see page 2) glass.
glass 150ml cocktail
garnish a small wedge of
lemon and a sprig of mint

mimosa

10ml orange curaçao
30ml fresh orange juice
90ml chilled
   brut champagne

Combine curaçao and
juice in a flute; top with
chilled champagne.
glass 150ml
champagne flute
garnish a twist of orange rind

kir royale

30ml crème de cassis
100ml chilled
  brut champagne

Pour crème de cassis
into a chilled flute; top
with chilled champagne.
glass 150ml
champagne flute

passionate affair

For this cocktail we used canned passionfruit in syrup, which is available from supermarkets.

15ml passionfruit liqueur
10ml passionfruit in syrup
120ml chilled
    brut champagne

Combine passionfruit liqueur and passionfruit in a flute; top with chilled champagne.
glass 150ml champagne flute

fruity champagne

This drink has its origins in the classic Bellini but gains distinction when the grenadine hits the glass. You can peel and puree the peach a short time before you want to serve this cocktail if you mix in the lemon juice to prevent it discolouring.

½ medium peach, peeled,
    chopped coarsely
5ml fresh lemon juice
dash grenadine
90ml chilled
    brut champagne

Blend or process peach until smooth; you need 30ml of peach puree. Combine peach puree in a glass with lemon juice and grenadine; top with chilled champagne.
glass 150ml
champagne flute
garnish a lemon slice

sangria

From humble origins in Spain where it was devised as a long, cool drink to combat the summer heat, sangria has become a popular punch at pubs and parties all over the world. If you want to be authentic, use a dry Spanish wine. This recipe makes about four glasses of sangria.

750ml bottle dry red wine
30ml Cointreau
30ml Bacardi
30ml brandy
½ cup (110g) sugar
2 cinnamon sticks
½ medium orange, peeled, chopped coarsely
½ medium lemon, peeled, chopped coarsely
6 medium strawberries, chopped coarsely
1 cup ice cubes

Place ingredients in a large jug; stir until well combined, pour into glasses.
glass 250ml highball

the soft option

Take the soft option with these delicious non-alcoholic drinks perfect for any time of day or night.

europa's virginity

4 x 5cm pieces watermelon
½ cup crushed ice
60ml bottled apple juice
90ml lemonade

Combine watermelon and ice in jug of a blender; blend on high speed until smooth. Pour into glass; top up with apple juice and lemonade.

glass 300ml highball
garnish a straw

regency fruit cocktail

3 medium strawberries
½ medium banana
2 x 5cm pieces pineapple
60ml fresh orange juice
60ml bottled
    pineapple juice
1 cup crushed ice

Combine ingredients in jug of a blender; blend on high speed until smooth, pour into glass.

glass 300ml highball
garnish a strawberry and a straw

grenadine rickey

½ cup ice cubes
30ml grenadine
10ml fresh lime juice
180ml soda water

Combine ice, grenadine and lime juice in glass; top with soda, stir to blend.

glass 300ml highball
garnish a wedge of lime, a swizzle stick and a straw

liquid love

4 medium frozen
   strawberries
90ml cranberry juice
10ml sugar syrup
   (see page 3)
10ml fresh lime juice
1 cup crushed ice

Combine ingredients in
jug of a blender; blend on
high speed until smooth,
pour into glass.
glass 150ml cocktail
garnish a strawberry
and a straw

watermelon wonder

120ml cranberry
   blackcurrant juice
4 x 5cm pieces watermelon
10ml fresh lemon juice
60ml bottled apple juice

Combine ingredients in jug
of a blender; blend on high
speed until smooth, pour
into chilled glass.
glass 300ml highball
garnish a straw

citron crush

½ medium lime, cut into
   4 wedges
½ medium lemon, cut into
   4 wedges
2 tablespoons palm sugar
   or brown sugar
4 large fresh mint leaves, torn
1 cup crushed ice
120ml lemonade

Using a mortar and pestle
(or muddler), crush lime,
lemon, sugar and mint.
Place ice in glass; pour
in the fruit mixture, then
top with lemonade.
glass 180ml old-fashioned
garnish a straw

grapefruit twist

orange rind knot

chocolate curls

pineapple-leaf spear

curled red chillies

garnishes

These easy garnishes are a quick way to lend your cocktails the appearance of sophisticated chic.

twist of citrus rind
Using a small sharp knife or a vegetable peeler in a spiralling motion, peel a long, thin piece of citrus rind from fruit then cut the rind into thin strips. Place the rind in the glass, hooking one end of rind over rim of glass.

knot of citrus rind
Remove strips of rind from fruit using a small sharp knife or a vegetable peeler then cut rind into thin strips. Tie strips into knots – this releases fragrant oil from citrus peel – and drop into drink immediately.

chocolate curls
Spread melted chocolate onto a cold surface (such as marble); when set, drag a sharp knife over the surface of chocolate to make curls. Alternatively, drag a vegetable peeler along the side of a block of chocolate.

pineapple-leaf spear
Using small sharp knife, make a small cut in the bottom-centre of a pineapple leaf. Place cut spear on rim of glass.

curled chillies
Using small sharp knife, cut a cross in bottom end of chilli. Place chilli in bowl of iced water; stand for 5 minutes. Place curled chilli on rim of glass.

amaretto an Italian liqueur made from apricot seeds with a decided almond flavour.

angostura bitters the best-known brand of bitters; an aromatic essence of herbs, roots and bark.

apple schnapps an apple-flavoured version of the clear German spirit distilled from various grains or potatoes.

bacardi brand name of the original Cuban rum. We used Bacardi Carta Blanca, a clear refined rum aged in white oak.

baileys a liqueur made from cream, Irish whiskey and spirits.

bourbon authentic American whiskey originating in Bourbon County, Kentucky; it's made from at least 51% corn, and aged in charred oak for a minimum two years.

brandy a liqueur made from distilled fermented grapes. If made from any other fruit, the fruit type is included in the name, eg, apple brandy.

campari Italian brand of bitters; deep-red in colour and having a bittersweet orange taste.

champagne a light sparkling wine, made in France by the méthode champenoise. Labels indicate level of sweetness: brut is the driest; extra-dry is less dry; sec is sweet; and demi-sec is even sweeter.

coconut cream first pressing from grated coconut flesh; available in cans and cartons.

coconut syrup a mixture of sugar, water and artificial or natural coconut flavouring; we used Monin coconut syrup in this book, available from most liquor shops.

cointreau a French liqueur; clear orange-flavoured brandy.

cream

fresh (minimum fat content 35%) also known as pure cream and pouring cream; has no additives like commercially thickened cream.

thickened (minimum fat content 35%) a whipping cream containing a thickener.

crème de cacao a liqueur made from cocoa beans and vanilla. It comes in two colours, dark and white (clear).

crème de cassis a liqueur made from blackcurrants.

curaçao named after a Caribbean island, on which the oranges for the original blend of this liqueur were grown. The most common colour of curaçao is white (clear), but it is also made in orange, red, green and blue versions.

frangelico an Italian hazelnut-flavoured liqueur.

gin an un-aged clear spirit distilled from grain alcohol, juniper berries and herbs.

ginger beer available in both non-alcoholic and alcoholic versions; made of ginger, sugar, water and yeast.

grenadine originally made from pomegranates grown on Caribbean island, Grenada; a dark-red non-alcoholic sugar syrup used to sweeten and colour cocktails and desserts.

ice magic brand name for a fast-setting chocolate topping; available from supermarkets.

kahlua a brandy-based liqueur flavoured with coffee.

lemon sorbet also known as sherbet or granita.

limoncello Italian lemon-flavoured liqueur.

malibu brand name of a rum-based coconut liqueur.

midori green Japanese liqueur made from honeydew melon.

oreo biscuits brand name of an American "cookie"; two small round chocolate biscuits enclosing a creme filling.

palm sugar a dark brown to black sugar from the coconut palm, sold in cakes; also known as gula jawa, gula melaka and jaggery.

rum a distillation of fermented sugar cane; colour varies from white (clear) to dark.

scotch whisky made in Scotland from a distillation of malted or unmalted barley dried with peat smoke and matured in oak at least three years.

tabasco sauce brand name of a fiery sauce made from vinegar, red peppers and salt.

tequila made from mixture of fresh and fermented agave juice (pulque); double-distilled to produce white (clear) tequila. Gold tequila is aged in oak casks for up to four years.

triple sec strong, white (clear), orange-flavoured liqueur similar to curaçao.

vermouth a herb-flavoured fortified white wine available dry (white) and sweet (bianco or rosso).

vodka an un-aged clear spirit distilled from grains such as barley, wheat or rye; also available in various citrus flavours.

worcestershire sauce thin, dark-brown spicy sauce used as a flavouring.

conversion chart

MEASURES

One Australian metric measuring cup holds approximately 250ml, one Australian metric tablespoon holds 20ml, one Australian metric teaspoon holds 5ml.

The difference between one country's measuring cups and another's is within a 2- or 3-teaspoon variance, and will not affect your cooking results. North America, New Zealand and the United Kingdom use a 15ml tablespoon. All cup and spoon measurements are level. The most accurate way of measuring dry ingredients is to weigh them. When measuring liquids, use a clear glass or plastic jug with metric markings.

We use large eggs with an average weight of 60g.

DRY MEASURES

METRIC	IMPERIAL
15g	½oz
30g	1oz
60g	2oz
90g	3oz
125g	4oz (¼lb)
155g	5oz
185g	6oz
220g	7oz
250g	8oz (½lb)
280g	9oz
315g	10oz
345g	11oz
375g	12oz (¾lb)
410g	13oz
440g	14oz
470g	15oz
500g	16oz (1lb)
750g	24oz (1½lb)
1kg	32oz (2lb)

LIQUID MEASURES

METRIC	IMPERIAL
30ml	1 fluid oz
60ml	2 fluid oz
100ml	3 fluid oz
125ml	4 fluid oz
150ml	5 fluid oz (¼ pint/1 gill)
190ml	6 fluid oz
250ml	8 fluid oz
300ml	10 fluid oz (½ pint)
500ml	16 fluid oz
600ml	20 fluid oz (1 pint)
1000ml (1 litre)	1¾ pints

LENGTH MEASURES

METRIC	IMPERIAL
3mm	⅛in
6mm	¼in
1cm	½in
2cm	¾in
2.5cm	1in
5cm	2in
6cm	2½in
8cm	3in
10cm	4in
13cm	5in
15cm	6in
18cm	7in
20cm	8in
23cm	9in
25cm	10in
28cm	11in
30cm	12in (1ft)

OVEN TEMPERATURES

These oven temperatures are only a guide for conventional ovens. For fan-forced ovens, check the manufacturer's manual.

	°C (CELSIUS)	°F (FAHRENHEIT)	GAS MARK
Very slow	120	250	½
Slow	150	275 – 300	1 – 2
Moderately slow	160	325	3
Moderate	180	350 – 375	4 – 5
Moderately hot	200	400	6
Hot	220	425 – 450	7 – 8
Very hot	240	475	9

index

Are you missing some of the world's favourite cookbooks?

The Australian Women's Weekly cookbooks are available from bookshops, cookshops, supermarkets and other stores all over the world. You can also buy direct from the publisher, using the order form below.

MINI SERIES £3.50 190x138MM 64 PAGES

TITLE	QTY	TITLE	QTY	TITLE	QTY
4 Fast Ingredients		Dried Fruit & Nuts		Party Food	
15-minute Feasts		Drinks		Pasta	
30-minute Meals		Fast Food for Friends		Pickles and Chutneys	
50 Fast Chicken Fillets		Fast Soup		Potatoes	
50 Fast Desserts (Oct 06)		Finger Food		Risotto	
After-work Stir-fries		Gluten-free Cooking		Roast	
Barbecue		Healthy Everyday Food 4 Kids		Salads	
Barbecue Chicken		Ice-creams & Sorbets		Simple Slices	
Barbecued Seafood		Indian Cooking		Simply Seafood	
Biscuits, Brownies & Biscotti		Indonesian Favourites		Skinny Food	
Bites		Italian		Spanish Favourites	
Bowl Food		Italian Favourites		Stir-fries	
Burgers, Rösti & Fritters		Jams & Jellies		Summer Salads	
Cafe Cakes		Japanese Favourites		Tapas, Antipasto & Mezze	
Cafe Food		Kids Party Food		Thai Cooking	
Casseroles		Last-minute Meals		Thai Favourites	
Char-grills & Barbecues		Lebanese Cooking		The Fast Egg	
Cheesecakes, Pavlova & Trifles		Low Fat Fast		The Packed Lunch	
Chinese Favourites		Malaysian Favourites		Vegetarian	
Chocolate Cakes		Mince		Vegetarian Stir-fries	
Christmas Cakes & Puddings		Mince Favourites		Vegie Main Meals	
Cocktails		Muffins		Wok	
Crumbles & Bakes		Noodles		Young Chef	
Curries		Outdoor Eating		TOTAL COST	£

Photocopy and complete coupon below

Name _____

Address _____

_____ Postcode _____

Country _____ Phone (business hours) _____

Email*(optional) _____

* *By including your email address, you consent to receipt of any email regarding this magazine, and other emails which inform you of ACP's other publications, products, services and events, and to promote third party goods and services you may be interested in.*

I enclose my cheque/money order for £ _____ or please charge £ _____

to my: ☐ Access ☐ Mastercard ☐ Visa ☐ Diners Club
PLEASE NOTE: WE DO NOT ACCEPT SWITCH OR ELECTRON CARDS

Card number | | | | | | | | | | | | | | | | |

3 digit security code *(found on reverse of card)* _____

Cardholder's
signature _____ Expiry date ____ /____

To order: Mail or fax – photocopy or complete the order form above, and send your credit card details or cheque payable to: Australian Consolidated Press (UK), Moulton Park Business Centre, Red House Road, Moulton Park, Northampton NN3 6AQ, phone (+44) (01) 604 497531, fax (+44) (01) 604 497533, e-mail books@acpmedia.co.uk. Or order online at www.acpuk.com
Non-UK residents: We accept the credit cards listed on the coupon, or cheques, drafts or International Money Orders payable in sterling and drawn on a UK bank. Credit card charges are at the exchange rate current at the time of payment.
All pricing current at time of going to press and subject to change/availability.
Postage and packing UK: Add £1.00 per order plus 25p per book.
Postage and packing overseas: Add £2.00 per order plus 50p per book. **Offer ends 31.12.2007**